Whatever
is
lovely

STAMP
HERE

Finally, brothers and sisters, whatever is true, whatever is noble, whatever is right, whatever is pure, whatever is lovely, whatever is admirable—if anything is excellent or praiseworthy—think about such things.

—PHILIPPIANS 4:8

Whatever is lovely

Jesus said, "Peace be with you! As the Father has sent me, I am sending you."

—JOHN 20:21

Illustrated by Linda A. Tetmyer; hand-lettered by Jennifer Tucker
From *Whatever Is Lovely*, © 2015 by WaterBrook

Whatever *is* lovely

Now then, my children, listen to me;
blessed are those who keep my ways.

—PROVERBS 8:32

Whatever is lovely

May we love big, walk bravely, speak truth.

—NISH WEISETH

I am with you always.

MATTHEW 28:20

Whatever is lovely

I am with you always, to the very end of the age.

—MATTHEW 28:20

Illustrated by Bridget Hurley; hand-lettered by Holly Camp
From *Whatever Is Lovely*, © 2015 by WaterBrook

Love NEVER gives up.

1 CORINTHIANS 13 (MSG)

No matter what I say, what I believe, and what I do,
I'm bankrupt without love. Love never gives up.

—1 CORINTHIANS 13:3–4 (MSG)

love defies expectation

Rachel Held Evans

Love bears expectations.

—RACHEL HELD EVANS

Whatever is lovely

Do not worry about tomorrow.

Matthew 6:34

Whatever is Lovely

Therefore do not worry about tomorrow, for tomorrow will worry about itself. Each day has enough trouble of its own.

—MATTHEW 6:34

Illustrated by Linda A. Tetmyer; hand-lettered by Jennifer Tucker
From *Whatever Is Lovely*, © 2015 by WaterBrook

May we be sensitive to the ways our words land in the hearts of others.

EMILY P. FREEMAN

May we be sensitive to the ways our words land in the hearts of others.

—EMILY P. FREEMAN IN *SIMPLY TUESDAY*

THE MOON SHINES FULL AT HIS COMMAND, AND ALL THE STARS OBEY. —ISAAC WATTS

I sing the wisdom that ordained the sun to rule the day;
The moon shines full at God's command, and all the stars obey.

—ISAAC WATTS

Whatever is lovely

it is well with my soul

HORATIO G. SPAFFORD

Whatever is Lovely

It is well, with my soul,
It is well, it is well with my soul.

—HORATIO G. SPAFFORD

So be truly glad

there is wonderful joy ahead

1 Peter 1:6 (NLT)

So be truly glad. There is wonderful joy ahead, even though you must endure many trials for a little while. These trials will show that your faith is genuine.

—1 PETER 1:6–7 (NLT)

Whatever is Lovely

LET YOUR GENTLENESS BE EVIDENT.
– PHILIPPIANS 4:5

Rejoice in the Lord always. I will say it again:
Rejoice! Let your gentleness be evident to all.

—PHILIPPIANS 4:4–5

Whatever is lovely

STAMP
HERE

A shelter in the time of storm

Vernon J. Charlesworth

Whatever is Lovely

Oh, Jesus is a Rock in a weary land,
A Shelter in the time of storm.

—VERNON J. CHARLESWORTH

Illustrated by Katherine Howe; hand-lettered by Jennifer Tucker
From *Whatever Is Lovely*, © 2015 by WaterBrook

gracious words are a honeycomb sweet to the soul and healing to the bones

PROVERBS 16:24

Whatever is Lovely

Gracious words are a honeycomb,
sweet to the soul and healing to the bones.

—PROVERBS 16:24

STAMP
HERE

Whatever is Lovely

Amazing grace! How sweet the sound
That saved a wretch like me!

—JOHN NEWTON

WE CAN PUT GOD FIRST
BY GIVING HIM OUR

FIRST MOMENTS

OF THE DAY.

LYSA TERKEURST

Whatever *is* lovely

We can put God first by giving Him our
first moments of the day.

—LYSA TERKEURST

Oh
for grace
to trust
Him more!

- LOUISA M.R. STEAD -

Jesus, Jesus, how I trust Him!
How I've proved Him o'er and o'er;
Jesus, Jesus, precious Jesus!
Oh, for grace to trust Him more!

—LOUISA M.R. STEAD

Whatever is lovely

STAMP
HERE

Be still
and
know that
I am God.
Psalm 46:10

I Whatever is Lovely

Be still, and know that I am God; I will be exalted among the nations, I will be exalted in the earth.

—PSALM 46:10

Illustrated by Bridget Hurley; hand-lettered by Jennifer Tucker
From *Whatever Is Lovely*, © 2015 by WaterBrook

HOW YOU FEEL
DOES NOT CHANGE
THE TRUTH OF THIS:
YOU ARE LOVED,
LOVED, LOVED.

—SARAH BESSEY

Whatever is Lovely

How you feel does not change the truth of this:
You are loved, loved, loved.

—SARAH BESSEY

YOU
WHO ARE
WEARY,
COME
HOME.

- WILL L. THOMPSON -

Come home, come home,
You who are weary, come home.

—WILL L. THOMPSON

whatever is lovely

Let all things their Creator bless

St. Francis of Assisi

Let all things their Creator bless,
And worship Him in humbleness,
O praise Him! Alleluia!

—ST. FRANCIS OF ASSISI

Whatever is lovely

STAMP
HERE

the One
who names the stars
Calls you by name
and calls you
His.

Liz
Curtis
Higgs

N
E
W
S

Whatever is Lovely

The One who names the stars calls you by name and calls you His.

—LIZ CURTIS HIGGS

He has made EVERYTHING beautiful in its time.

Ecclesiastes 3:11

Whatever is Lovely

He has made everything beautiful in its time. He has also set eternity in the human heart; yet no one can fathom what God has done from beginning to end.

—ECCLESIASTES 3:11

Illustrated by Jennifer Tucker. From *Whatever Is Lovely*, © 2015 by WaterBrook